MY COUNTRY

Muhammad Haji Salleh

Art by Shafrudin

My Country
begins with the high clouds
and ends as waves striking the bows.

My Country
wakes up as a drop of dew
and retires a school of fireflies.

My Country
flows from a drop of rain
and ends as a red estuary.

My Country
stretches on the green of forests
and ends on the yellow carpet of paddy.

My Country
is surrounded by the seas
stopping only at the sun!

RAIN
OF THE WORLD

A Gujarati Folk song

Art by Albert Bierstadt

Pour down, O Rain of the World,
You are the rain of four continents,
The earth, your beloved is waiting for you.

The happy farmers are waiting for you,
The plough bullocks are waiting for you,
Your loved people are waiting for you.

Pour down O Rain of the World,
The birds and beasts are waiting for you,
Rivers and trees are all waiting for you.

Pour down, O Dark Clouds, pour down,
And fill the ponds and lakes with water,
Bring happiness and joy to the world.

THE NORTHERN LIGHTS

Kalli Dakos

Photo by Johannes Frank

The northern lights
put on a show
in the polar sky.
They pranced,
they danced,
kept us entranced,
a whirlwind up high.
The colours streamed
in blues and greens
with rosy red rays.

They lit the night
with wild light
across the Milky Way.
We couldn't run.
We couldn't play.
We couldn't even speak.
In a daze,
we just gazed
till our legs went weak.
Faraway
we heard the bell,
to call us back inside.
We didn't move.
We were glued,
to the wonders in the sky!

The Northern Lights are mysteries of Earth!
Can climate change affect the lights?

Scientists say Yes!

THE BIG OLD ENOKI TREE

There was once a young man. His name was Satsuma. He lived in a garden, that was more beautiful than any that you have ever seen. It had many trees with flowers and buds and fruits. Ponds and little lakes. And a tall and spreading enoki tree.

The enoki was a very, very old tree. Some people said it was a thousand years old!

Satsuma was a man with a very bad heart. He said, "I can't see the sun when I wake up in the morning, because of that tree." So he called a lot of men and cut down the tree.

Strangely, that day, Satsuma fell ill. And from that day on, he never came out of his house at all. And there was no one to look after Satsuma's house and garden.

A Japanese Folktale
Art by Rumi Hara

One day, a girl called Tikem saw the tall dark walls of the strange garden that no one ever went to. She boldly walked into the cold, unhappy place. She spoke to the trees. She touched them with loving hands.

Days and years went by. Tikem went to the garden every day.

Slowly … people in the village saw a strange thing. A small enoki tree growing in the place of the old enoki!

Every year, as if by magic, the tree grew. And grew. And grew. Soon the birds and the bees came back. So did the flowers and fruits on the trees in the garden.

Soon, children of the village played happily in the butterfly garden.

Tikem's smile was like sunshine putting little stars on each branch of each tree.

Satsuma saw this. And his heart filled with sadness. How unfair he had been to the old enoki tree. To the children of his village. Even to himself!

Slowly, he walked out of his house into the beautiful garden Tikem had made … And slowly, he became the boy he once was.

Tikem and Satsuma now together look after their beautiful garden. With the children of the village. The birds. And the flowers. And the little enoki which would live and grow with the village, for a thousand years!

Art by Franz Marc

HOW COW?

There are 150 crore cattle in the world. Researchers say there is a link beween cattle and climate change.

CURIOUS?

Find your answer after two pages!

Women!

Geeta Dharmarajan

Art by Alison Dunnell

Who brings water to the family, everyday?
For everyone to bathe and wash, to cook and
quench their thirst?

Women and girls, mostly!

Many of them spend many many hours
searching for water. And walking to and from
these distant places where they find water.

think

Water is life! But global climate change is going to make
safe water even more difficult to get for all of us on Earth!
So what is Climate Change?

Turn the page to find out!

PLANET EARTH IS AWESOME!

BUT EARTH WILL NOT BE THE SAME IF WE DON'T DO SOMETHING ...

- The Northern Lights will disappear and the butterflies too, because the climate is changing!
- Countries will lose their animals and plants, because the climate is changing!
- Rain will not pour enough, and we won't have enough water, because the climate is changing!
- And the climate is changing mainly because we, as humans, don't care!

HOW COW?

Research shows that rearing cattle for meat is taking up too much land and resources than food crops.

So, we cut more trees. We increase the amount of CO_2 in the air. Animals like cows also release methane gas in digesting their food.

Scientists say that increase in these gases in the air is leading to climate change.

> **" I don't want to be thought of as the girl who was shot by the Taliban but the girl who fought for education. This is the cause to which I want to devote my life. "**

MALALA FOUND HER VOICE! SHE SPOKE UP WHEN SHE WAS NOT ABLE TO GO TO SCHOOL IN PAKISTAN!

FIND YOUR VOICE NOW!

Speak up for Planet Earth! Write a letter to our Prime Minister, asking for a ban on tree cutting to help Mother Earth.

1. Visit http://www.pmindia.gov.in/
2. Scroll down. Find this: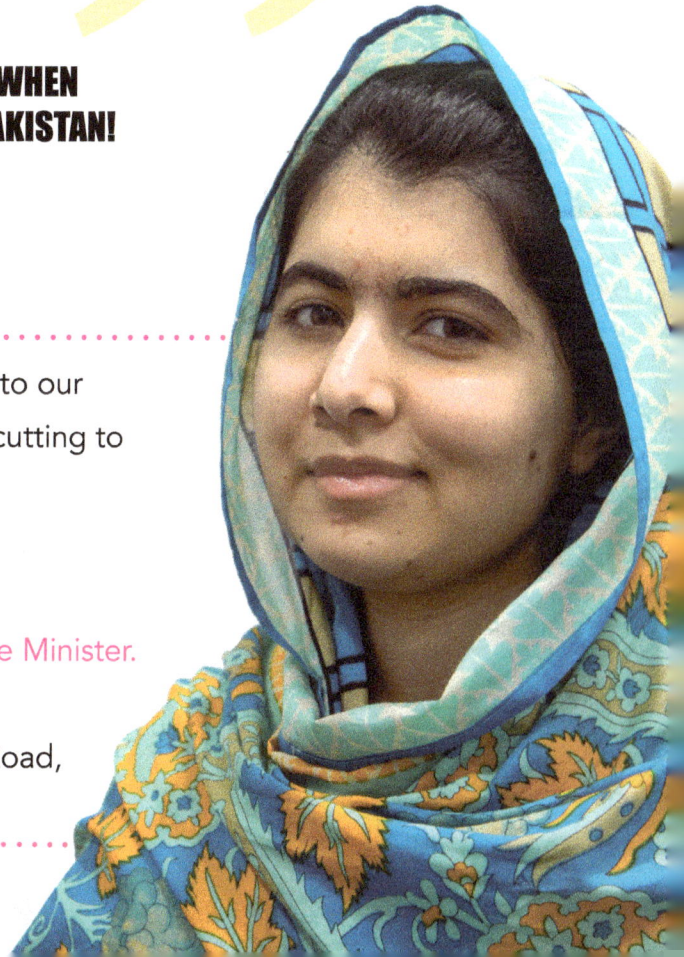
3. Click on this logo. Write To The Prime Minister.
4. Or send your handwritten letter to:
   The Prime Minister, 7, Race Course Road,
   New Delhi - 110011

Art by Suddhasattwa Basu

So what is this terrible thing called

CLIMATE CHANGE

And why should you care?

Guha Dharmarajan

 **Before we talk about climate change let us talk about the moon.**

Did you know that the moon can get very very cold. Or really boiling hot! The temperature can range between –173°C and 127°C ?

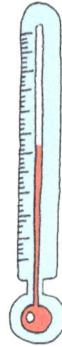 Remember water freezes at 0oC and boils at 100oC.

So why doesn't the earth get so cold or hot?

The answer is: **Air.**

Yes, the thing you can't see but must breathe to live. The thing that carries Amma's voice calling you home for dinner. And the thing that carries the smell of hot chapatis to your nose!

Air is important for us to live.

So why is air so important for the Earth's temperature?

The reason is that air can trap heat. It is a good insulator.

If you live in a cold area you would use a razai. The razai is a good insulator. When we fluff up the cotton before winter, the cotton traps air. So, the fluffier the cotton, the more air gets trapped. And the warmer the razai will keep you.

Art by Charbak Dipta

Scientists call air, atmosphere.

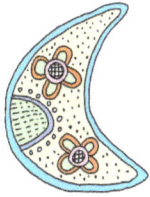

The moon has no atmosphere. So the surface of the moon that is facing the sun gets very hot and the surface away from the sun gets very cold.

The earth has an atmosphere. This atmosphere keeps the earth from getting too hot or too cold by acting like a "greenhouse."

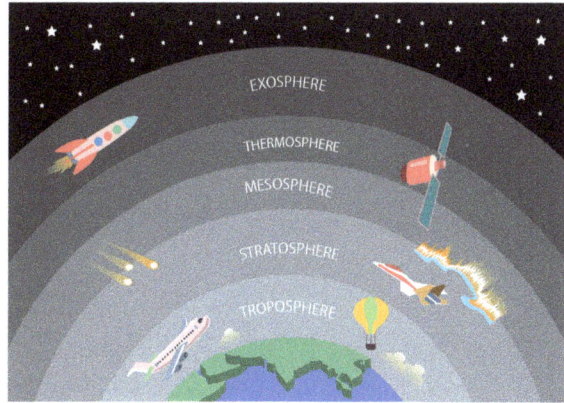

The Earth's Atmosphere

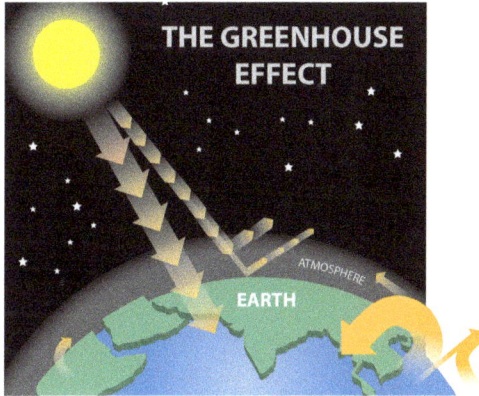

What is a greenhouse?

A greenhouse is a special house for plants. It has glass walls and a glass roof. People in cold countries grow vegetables and flowers in them.

Why? Because the sun shines through the glass and keeps the inside air warm, even during winter. And because of the glass, the heat cannot escape. So during the day, it gets warmer and warmer inside a greenhouse. And stays warm at night too.

The earth's atmosphere works like a greenhouse.

Gases like carbon dioxide (CO_2) act like the "roof" of the greenhouse. During the day the sun shines through the atmosphere. The Earth's layer traps some of the heat, like your razai, and the surface warms up. At night, Earth's surface cools, and the heat escapes back into the atmosphere. Some of the heat is trapped by CO_2 and other gases. This is what keeps our Earth nice and cozy!

TOO COLD   **TOO HOT**

Too hot? Too cold?

As you can imagine, there is a fine balance between trapping too little heat (in which case the earth will be too cold for us to live in) and trapping too much heat (in which case the earth will get too hot to live in.)

Today, scientists are concerned about the atmosphere trapping too much heat. Why? Because many things that we humans do, lead to an increase in the CO_2 in the atmosphere.

CO_2 and other greenhouse gases trap heat in Earth's atmosphere

Is CO_2 bad?

Carbon dioxide can absorb and release a lot of heat while oxygen is very poor at this job. That is why CO_2 is called a "greenhouse gas."

Carbon dioxide is a natural part of the earth's atmosphere. As you know from your science lesson, it is important for life on Earth.

But scientists are very worried because we humans are releasing more CO_2 than is good for our planet.

As more and more CO_2 is released, it helps the atmosphere hold more and more heat.

This effect is called **Global Warming.**

Burn fossil fuels: Fossil fuels are the remains of plants or animals that have stayed very deep under the ground for thousands of years. Oil, coal, petrol, diesel, natural gas are forms of fossil fuels. When we burn fossil fuels we release CO_2.

Cut down trees: Trees absorb and remove CO_2 from the air. When we cut down forests, we rob Earth of a way to absorb CO_2. Burning trees also releases CO_2.

Use electricity: We make electricity mainly with fossil fuels today, for example, through burning coal.

WE PRODUCE MORE CO_2 THAN IS GOOD FOR US, WHEN WE ...

Over Use Motorbikes, cars, buses, trucks, large ships, aeroplanes and rockets which release CO_2.

Don't REDUCE. REUSE. RECYCLE.

Build with cement, iron or steel. These industries need a HUGE amount of heat energy to convert raw materials into construction products. This produces a LOT of CO_2.

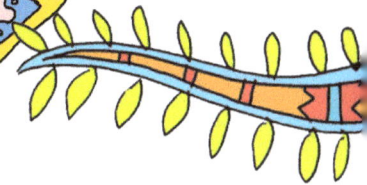

Is global warming the same as climate change?

Remember that the term global warming means that scientists expect that the temperature on Earth will gradually keep on increasing as the years go by. It will be so slow, that we may not even notice it.

And when global warming keeps happening as humans produce more and more CO_2, weather patterns change a lot, making climate across the world change.

And as the world gets warmer, more of the ice in the Arctic and Antarctic will melt.

Where will all this water go?

Into our oceans leading to rise in sea levels.

So, if you live on the coast, scientists think houses and lands will get swallowed up by the sea. And people will die, unless we can breathe under water! The United Nations estimates that crores of Indians will be at risk from sea level rise over the next 30 years.

Climate change can have many other effects on humans and animals.

SEA LEVEL

WHY IS GLOBAL WARMING DANGEROUS?

Plants & Animals will die. Many animals and plants and farmer's crops around the world may not be able to adapt to the climatic change and can die or lose their homes.

And when trees and animals die, we human beings will follow. We need them to live!

Sea levels rise. We could have more storms. Floods. Drought. Hurricanes and tsunamis. Some parts of the Earth will get less rain. Others will get much more.

Agriculture. Experts say that in places like India, we may not be able to produce much grains or crops. Livestock may die due to heat and drought.

And where it is going to be wetter and colder, there would be more floods and tsunamies. And so they may not be able to grow much food either.

Health. Sickness, deaths from water borne diseases, from heat waves or cold waves, and those caused by rats and other rodents will increase. Mosquitoes and other insects will increase. Diseases like malaria will become common. And you know they are life-threatening!

I am sure you are already seeing some effects of climate change in your hometown. It has a major effect on crops and weather.

Is our climate changing now?

Yes! India needs the monsoons for agriculture. And even now we see how undependable the monsoons are. And monsoons will get more unpredictable as climate change worsens.

But the effects of global warming will be seen as summers grow hotter. Winters get colder. There will be too much rain and floods. Or too little rain. And parched earth and droughts.

This is why scientists today use the term "Climate Change" to describe what is happening to the earth due to human activities.

Global warming is a serious problem but you can do little things to be an earth-carer. Start today!

THINK: Are you already seeing the effects of climate change in your home town?

ASK: Your grandmother. Does she think that the climate has got more variable now than when she was a child?

DISCUSS: What can we do as Earth-carers?

See opposite page for some great ideas!

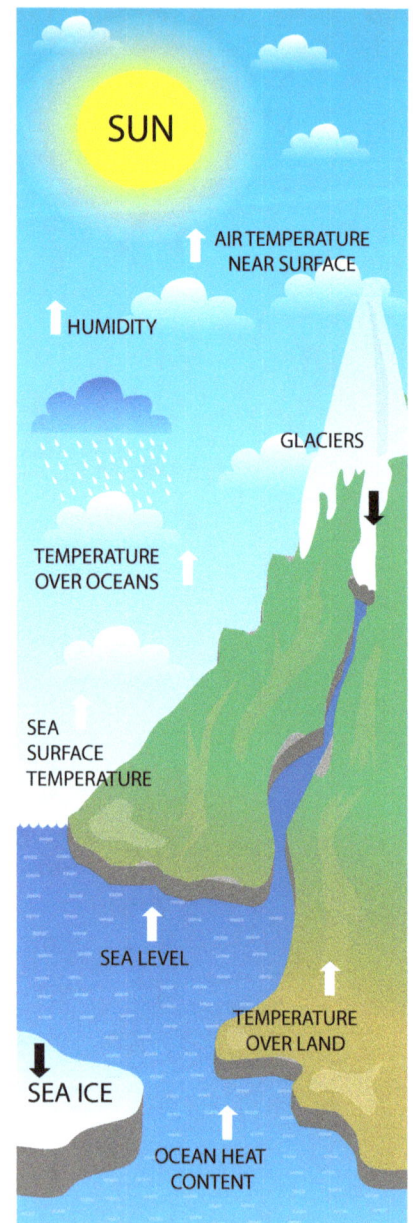

SUN

AIR TEMPERATURE NEAR SURFACE

HUMIDITY

GLACIERS

TEMPERATURE OVER OCEANS

SEA SURFACE TEMPERATURE

SEA LEVEL

TEMPERATURE OVER LAND

SEA ICE

OCEAN HEAT CONTENT

Impact of Global Warming on Earth
↑ indicates increasing levels
↓ indicates decreasing levels

WHAT YOU CAN DO!

Try to make less use of electrical items such as geysers, heaters, exhaust fans and air conditioners as they consume a lot of electricty.

Use a bicycle for short distances. And you get exercise too:)

Use as little electricity as you can! Turn off electrical things like computers, fans and lights when not using them or when you leave the room.

Drive your car less. Take the school bus when you can. Or walk!

And most importantly! Plant trees! This is a great way to reduce greenhouse gases. Trees absorb carbon dioxide, a greenhouse gas, from the air.

Our Sun is a good source of energy. Use solar energy whenever you can. Government has schemes where they help you get cheaper solar panels. Check with your local government.

Use glass bottles, and cloth or paper bags. These can be used again. Or recycled. Please do not use plastic bottles or bags.

Global warming is the greatest environmental challenge of the 21st century. So ... let us be kind to Mother Earth!

If I can STOP

Emily Dickinson

Art by Falguni Gokhale

If I can stop one heart from breaking,

I shall not live in vain;

If I can ease one life the aching,

Or cool one pain,

Or help one fainting robin

Unto his nest again,

I shall not live in vain.

A PAGE FOR YOU TO COLOUR

Out of this world experiences
Just for you:))

THINK
If you were to put
up a play for forest dwellers —
birds, animals, trees, what
would you tell them about
global climate change??

BE A DETECTIVE!
Take a photo of a sound
that could have been heard
1,000 years ago.

DISCUSS
Sit with your friends to discuss the best way to save Earth just where you live.

ACT!
Now ... Choose an animal character to think like. Make a mask for yourself of this character or anything else. You could be a squirrel, an ant or a tree!

And go on an adventure!

REMEMBER!
When you put on the mask, you must think and feel like the character you are playing!

Albert Bierstadt was a German painter who loved travelling and painting mountain landscapes. | **Alison Dunnell** is an artist, photographer and teacher who travels the world recording images of people and life in sketchbooks, canvases and online. | **Emily Dickinson** was an ingenious poet known for her enigmatic brilliance and style. She was not publicly recognized during her lifetime as most of her work was published posthumously after she died in 1886. | **Falguni Gokhale** is an artist by passion and a visual communication designer, by profession. She is the co-owner of Design Directions. | **Franz Marc** was a German painter. He used a lot of bold and bright colours for his paintings and loved to draw animals. | **Guha Dharmarajan** is research scientist, disease ecologist, a veterinarian and an animal lover. He lives with his cat, Maximus, in Aiken. | **Johannes Frank** is a self-taught photographer who feels connected with and inspired by nature. | "A poem can change a child, and a child can change the world," said **Kalli Dakos**, a Canadian writer, poet, teacher and a reading specialist. | **Muhammad Haji Salleh** is Malaysia's best-known bilingual writer and has twelve volumes of poetry published since his commencement as a writer in 1963. | **Rumi Hara** is an illustrator and comics artist. | **Shafrudin** is an artist from Malaysia. | **Suddhasattwa Basu** is a renowned illustrator, painter and maker of animation films for television.

First published by Katha, 2019
Copyright © Katha, 2019
Text copyright © Respective Authors
Paintings copyright © Respective Artists
All rights reserved. No part of this book may be reproduced or utilized in any form without the prior written permission of the publisher.
ISBN 978-93-88284-16-5
E-mail: marketing@katha.org, Website: www.katha.org

Our Mission: Every child reading well for fun and meaning! KATHA is a registered nonprofit organization started in 1988. We work in the literacy to literature continuum. Devoted to enhancing the joys of reading amongst children and adults, we work with more than 1,00,000 children in poverty, to bring them to grade-level reading through quality books and interventions.
A3, Sarvodaya Enclave, Sri Aurobindo Marg, New Delhi 110 017
Phone: 4141 6600 . 4182 9998 . 2652 1752

This book is supported by Embassy of Federal Republic of Germany, New Delhi.

Ten per cent of sales proceeds from this book will support the quality education of children studying in Katha Schools. Katha regularly plants trees to replace the wood used in the making of its books.

These books are specially made with love and care by the Katha team, for 5-12 year olds.

They are part of our UntextBook Initiative, to bring the joy of reading through literature and fabulous artworks.

Take your child from wordless books to books with 1200 words. 13 Thinkbooks in each level. Five levels of handpicked literature.

Stories and poems from 3,500 years of literary history. And the best of art – from MF Hussain to van Gogh to fab photographers.

Read with your child. Colour her world with imagination. Culturelinking.

Join the 300 Million Movement! Let us make our children proud!
To join: 300m@katha.org
To volunteer: volunteer@katha.org

I Love Reading library is a unique series of books that brings new and diffident readers into reading fluently. With high-quality content and design to match the learning needs of children who are at different reading levels, it brings together the finest literary creations and art works from India and the world. Our books manifest Geeta Dharmarajan's StoryPedagogy™ – a unique pedagogical model, which promotes the joy of reading specially for first generation readers and takes the child into the fascinating world of BIG Ideas and TA-DAA! (Think, Ask, Discuss, Act, and take Action).

Katha's Holistic Early Learning (KHEL!) Lab offers workshops to teachers in government, non-profit and private schools. These are F2F (Face-to-Face) workshops supported by online sessions leading to a "Reading Teacher's Certificate" for teachers, school administrators and volunteers. To know more, write to us at 300m@katha.org.

www.ingramcontent.com/pod-product-compliance
Lightning Source LLC
Chambersburg PA
CBHW041634040426
42447CB00020B/3488